yukismart.com/b/65ad76
AF365073
1
2

**girl**

**дівчинка**
*divchynka*

**boy**

**хлопчик**
*khlopchyk*

# mommy

## мама
*mama*

# daddy

## тато
*tato*

**young**

**молодий**
*molodyi*

**old**

**старий**
*staryi*

**child**

**дитина**
*dytyna*

**adult**

**дорослий**
*doroslyi*

## accept

**приймати**
*pryimaty*

## refuse

**відмовлятися**
*vidmovliatysia*

**yes**

**так**
*tak*

**no**

**ні**
*ni*

# smile

**посміхатися**
*posmikhatysia*

# cry

**плакати**
*plakaty*

# happy

**щасливий**
*shchaslyvyi*

# sad

**сумний**
*sumnyi*

**alone**

**один**
*odyn*

**together**

**разом**
*razom*

**noise**

**шум**
*shum*

**quiet**

**тиша**
*tysha*

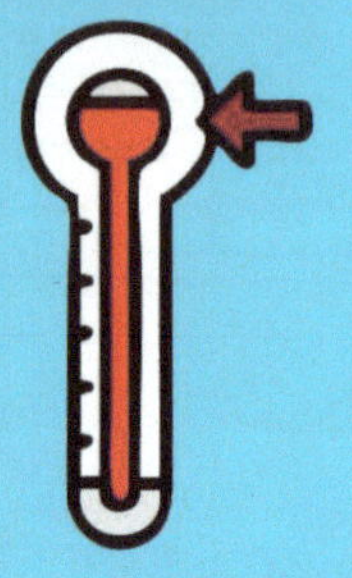

**hot**

**гарячий**
*hariachyi*

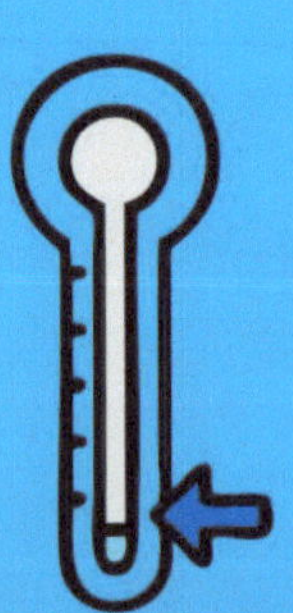

**cold**

**холодний**
*kholodnyi*

## a little

**трохи**
*trokhy*

## a lot

**багато**
*bahato*

## solid

**твердий**
*tverdyi*

## liquid

**рідкий**
*ridkyi*

## short

**короткий**
*korotkyi*

## long

**довгий**
*dovhyi*

## slow

**повільний**
*povilnyi*

## fast

**швидкий**
*shvydkyi*

## tiny

**крихітний**
*krykhitnyi*

## small

**маленький**
*malenkyi*

## big

**великий**
*velykyi*

## huge

**великий**
*velykyi*

**in**

**всередині**

*vseredyni*

**out**

**поза**

*poza*

**inflated**

**надутий**

*nadutyi*

**deflated**

**здутий**

*zdutyi*

**on**

**на**
*na*

**under**

**під**
*pid*

**dirty**

**брудний**

*brudnyi*

**clean**

**чистий**

*chystyi*

**identical**

**однаковий**

*odnakovyi*

**different**

**відмінний**

*vidminnyi*

**left**

ліво

*livo*

**right**

право

*pravo*

$$1 + 1 = 5$$

**wrong**

невірно

*nevirno*

$$1 + 1 = 2$$

**correct**

правильний

*pravylnyi*

## thin

**тонкий**
*tonkyi*

## thick

**товстий**
*tovstyi*

## easy

**легкий**
*lehkyi*

## difficult

**важко**
*vazhko*

**close**

**закритий**
*zakrytyi*

**open**

**відкритий**
*vidkrytyi*

# tall

## високий
*vysokyi*

# short

## низький
*nyzkyi*

**healthy**

**здоровий**
*zdorovyi*

**sick**

**хворий**
*khvoryi*

**day**

**день**
*den*

**night**

**ніч**
*nich*

**play**

**грати**
*hraty*

**sleep**

**спати**
*spaty*

## sunny

**сонячно**
*soniachno*

## cloudy

**хмарно**
*khmarno*

## rainy

**дощовий**
*doshchovyi*

## stormy

**бурхливий**
*burkhlyvyi*

**white**

білий

*bilyi*

**black**

чорний

*chornyi*

**light colors**

світлі кольори

*svitli kolory*

**dark colors**

темні кольори

*temni kolory*

**sweet**

**солодкий**
*solodkyi*

**sour**

**кислий**
*kyslyi*

**salty**

**солоний**
*solonyi*

**bitter**

**гіркий**
*hirkyi*

**whole**

**ціле**
*tsile*

**half**

**половина**
*polovyna*

**full**

**повний**
*povnyi*

**empty**

**пустий**
*pustyi*

**eat**

**їсти**
*isty*

**drink**

**пити**
*pyty*

**near**

**близько**
*blyzko*

**far**

**далеко**
*daleko*

there
там
tam

here
тут
tut

# stand up

**встати**
*vstaty*

# lay down

**лягти**
*liahty*

# sit down

**сідати**
*sidaty*

curly hair
кучеряве волосся
kucheriave volossia
straight hair
пряме волосся
priame volossia

**soaked**

**промоклий**
*promoklyi*

**wet**

**мокрий**
*mokryi*

**dry**

**сухий**
*sukhyi*

## in front of

**перед**
*pered*

## behind

**позаду**
*pozadu*

## between

**між**
*mizh*

## beside

**поряд з**
*poriad z*

## roof

**дах**
*dakh*

## floor

**підлога**
*pidloha*

**heavy**

**важкий**
*vazhkyi*

**light**

**легкий**
*lehkyi*

## fragile

**крихкий**
*krykhkyi*

## hardy

**міцний**
*mitsnyi*

## weak

**слабкий**
*slabkyi*

## strong

**сильний**
*sylnyi*

**sharp**

**гострий**
*hostryi*

**soft**

**м'який**
*m'iakyi*

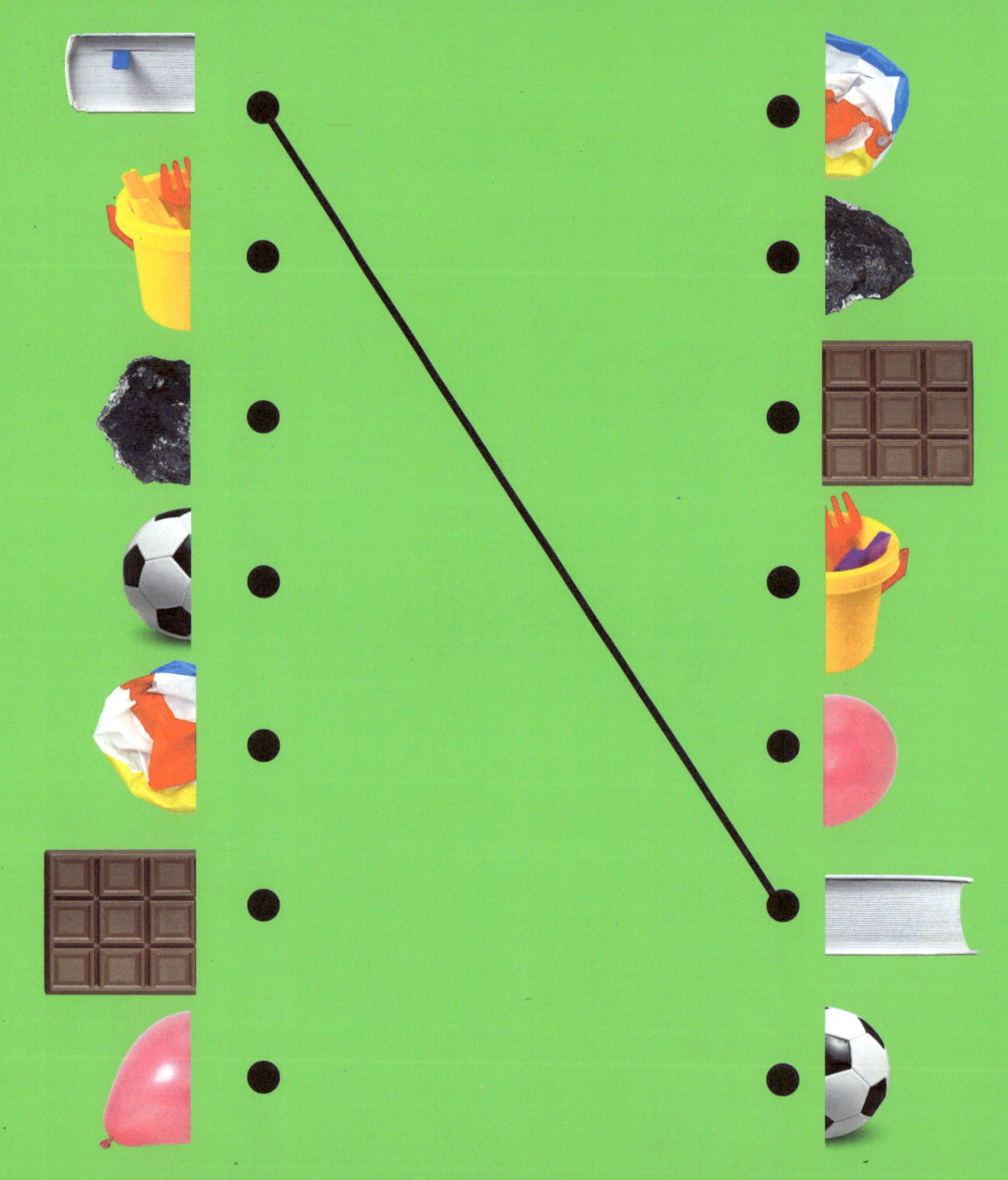